Nature's Wonders

THE GREAT LAKES

PATRICIA K. KUMMER

 **Marshall Cavendish**
Benchmark
New York

Marshall Cavendish Benchmark
99 White Plains Road
Tarrytown, NY 10591-5502
www.marshallcavendish.us

Expert Reader: Mark Coscarelli, Senior Consultant, Great Lakes and Environmental Policy,
Public Sector Consultants Inc., East Lansing, Michigan

All Internet addresses were correct and accurate at the time of printing.

Library of Congress Cataloging-in-Publication Data
Kummer, Patricia K.
The Great Lakes / by Patricia K. Kummer
p. cm. — (Nature's Wonders)
Summary: "Provides comprehensive information on the geography, history, wildlife, peoples,
and environmental issues of the Great Lakes"—Provided by publisher
Includes bibliographical references and index.
ISBN 978-0-7614-2853-4
1. Great Lakes (North America)—Juvenile literature. 2. Great Lakes Region
(North America)—Juvenile literature. I. Title.
F551.K86 2008
977—dc22
2007019728

Editor: Christine Florie
Publisher: Michelle Bisson
Art Director: Anahid Hamparian
Series Designer: Kay Petronio

Photo research by Connie Gardner

Cover photo by Ron Watts/First Light/Getty Images

The photographs in this book are used by permission and through the courtesy of:
North Wind Picture Archives: 1, 48, 53, 56-57, 58; *Peter Arnold:* BIOS Bios Auteurs Van, 3, 89 (B), Steven Kazlowski,
89 (T); *Granger Collection:* 88 (B); *Getty Images:* Chris Strong, 4; Ethan Mcleg, 10-11; Wayne R. Bilenduke, 45; Gary
Meszaros, 47; Henry Georgi, 76; Eddie Soloway, 88 (T); *Dembinsky Photo Associates:* NASA, 7; Willard Clambinsky,
14; G. Alan Nelson, 25; Dan Dempster, 32-33; Dominique Braud, 41; *Larry Ulrich:* Craig Blacklock, 12; *Corbis:*
Layne Kennedy, 15, 26, 29; Joseph Sohm, 18-19, 64-65; Bobbi Lane, 22; David Muench, 36; Sally A. Morgan,
42; Robert Pickett, 44; James Amos, 62, 69; Jose Fuste Raga, 66; Phil Schermeister, 70, 78; Rudy Sulgan, 72-
73; Charles Rotkin, 80; *The Image Works:* Joe Sohm, 68; Jeff Greenberg, 74, 85; Jim West, 82; Tannen Maury,
83; *Minden Pictures:* Jim Brandenburg, 34, 37; Mark Raycroft, 41; *Alamy:* Dennis MacDonald, 30; Mary Evans
Picture Library, 51; North Wind Picture Archives, 59; *age footstock:* Don Johnston, 20; *Super Stock:* Joe Vogan, 38.

Maps and food chain illustration by Mapping Specialists Limited.

Printed in China

1 3 5 6 4 2

CONTENTS

ONE

Sweet Water Seas

"Water, water, everywhere. Nor any drop to drink." This line from an English poem describes the predicament of an old mariner who is surrounded by undrinkable ocean water. About 75 percent of the earth's surface is covered by water and ice, but about 97 percent of that is saltwater in the world's oceans, seas, and some large lakes. About 2 percent of the earth's drinking water is frozen in the polar ice caps. That leaves only about 1 percent of the earth's surface water available as freshwater. Freshwater is sometimes referred to as "sweet water" to distinguish it from saltwater, from water that is **alkaline**, or from water that is in some other way polluted and undrinkable.

If the mariner in the poem had been on Lake Superior or on any of the other four Great Lakes, he could have dipped in his hand or a bucket and come up with "sweet," drinkable water. In fact, that is exactly what the French explorer Samuel de Champlain is said to have done in 1615. He thought Lake Huron might be another ocean. As a test Champlain scooped up a handful of water and put it to his mouth. He was surprised that it wasn't salty and exclaimed, "Ah, sweet water!" "Sweet Water Seas" has become one of the Great Lakes' nicknames.

◀ *The Great Lakes system is the largest source of fresh drinking water in the world.*

North America's five Great Lakes—Superior, Michigan, Huron, Erie, and Ontario—contain about 20 percent of the world's surface freshwater. Lake Superior by itself holds 10 percent of the world's freshwater. Of the world's twelve largest freshwater lakes the Great Lakes rank in total area from first (Lake Superior) to twelfth (Lake Ontario). Lake Huron ranks third; Michigan, fourth; and Lake Erie, tenth. The Great Lakes are the only large bodies of freshwater in a temperate climate where many people are able to live. The rest of the world's large freshwater lakes are in remote, frigid, Arctic areas or in the hot, humid tropics. Having a source of freshwater nearby is important for human beings for many reasons. The main reason is because water makes up about 60 percent of the body's weight and clean drinking water is necessary to sustain human life.

THE GREAT LAKES REGION

The Great Lakes are located in the northeastern part of the United States and in the southeastern part of Canada. Most of the eastern half of the U.S.–Canada border runs through four of the Great Lakes—Lakes Superior, Huron, Erie, and Ontario. Lake Michigan is the only Great Lake located entirely within the United States.

A satellite view of the Great Lakes shows the huge amount of surface area that they cover in North America.

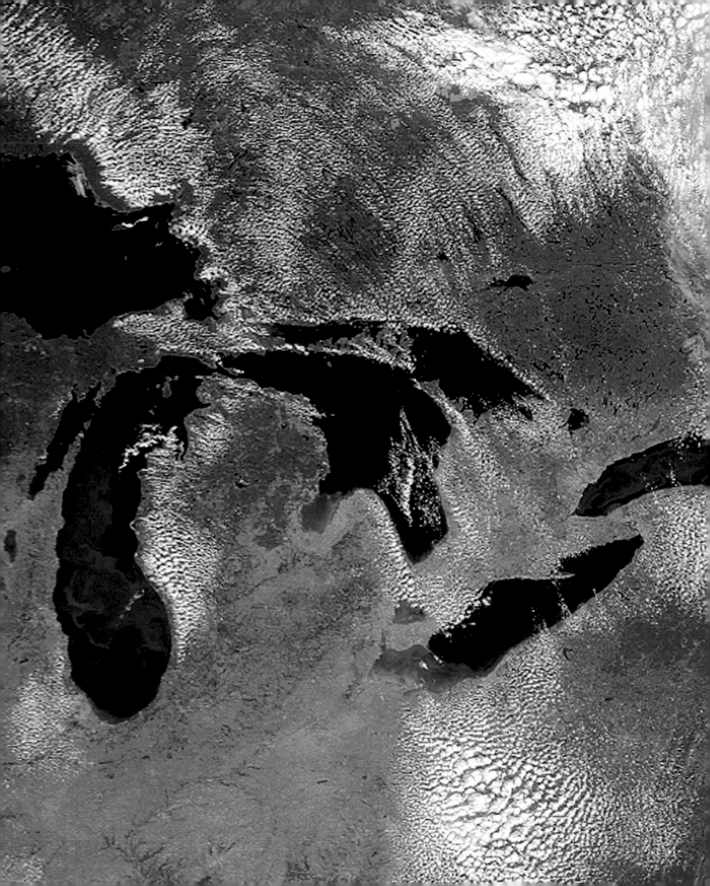

There's an easy way to remember the names of the five Great Lakes. It's the mnemonic **HOMES**. Each letter stands for the name of one of the Lakes—**H**uron, **O**ntario, **M**ichigan, **E**rie, **S**uperior. **HOMES** is often used as a crossword puzzle clue, and the answer is usually "Erie."

Because the five Great Lakes are each so large and are naturally connected to one another, they have a great effect on the vegetation and climate of the surrounding land. Parts of eight states—Minnesota, Wisconsin, Michigan, Illinois, Indiana, Ohio, Pennsylvania, and New York—and the Canadian province of Ontario border the Great Lakes. The land that borders the lakes and the lakes themselves make up the Great Lakes region. The state of Michigan is surrounded by four of the Great Lakes—Superior, Michigan, Huron, and a bit of Erie. That is why Michigan's nickname is "The Great Lakes State."

A REMARKABLE NATURAL WONDER

Most natural wonders are in isolated areas, far from heavily populated cities. Many natural wonders are best known for their beauty or

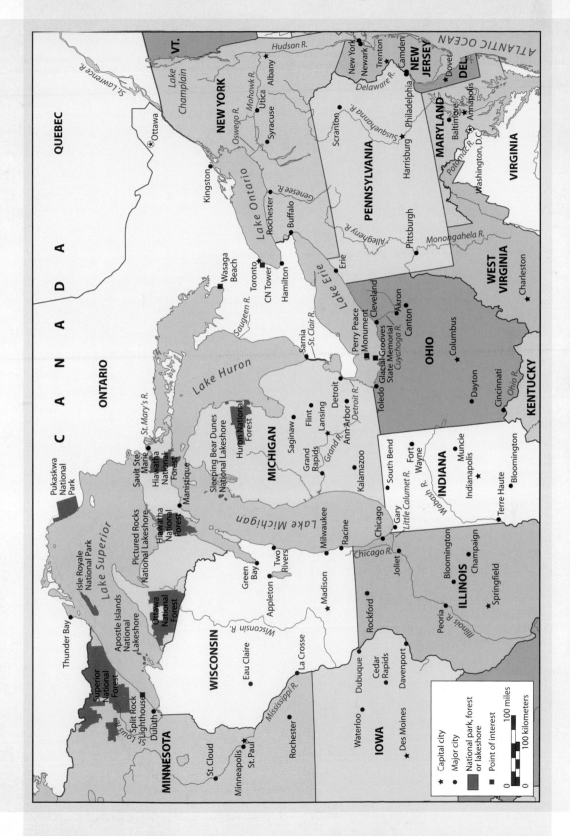

GEOPOLITICAL MAP OF THE GREAT LAKES

for something unusual about their appearance. Some of the world's natural wonders have "great" or "grand" as part of their names. The use of "great" and "grand" usually refers to an aspect of the wonder's physical dimensions, such as total area or depth, which is true of the Great Lakes. In fact, the lakes' large sizes make them one of only a few natural sites in North America that are visible from outer space. The Great Lakes and their natural resources have been the backbone of cultures, civilizations, and cities for hundreds of years. The most important of these natural resources is the freshwater itself, which provides drinking water for approximately forty million people in the region.

Besides their natural wonder, great beauty, and awesome size, the Great Lakes are also remarkable in other ways. First, Canada's largest city and several large U.S. cities are located along the Great Lakes. Second, the lakes create the world's largest and busiest inland waterway for ships. Third, these ships call on some of North America's busiest ports, which are located on the Great Lakes. Fourth, the Great Lakes provide recreational activities for more than five million people every year. Fifth and perhaps most important, the lakes are not only a natural wonder but a natural resource—the world's largest source of sweet, drinkable freshwater.

The Great Lakes are not only a source of drinking water, but also are economic and recreational resources.

TWO

The Fourth Coast

Another of the Great Lakes' nicknames is "The Fourth Coast." The three other coasts that touch North America, as well as land of the United States, are formed by the Atlantic and Pacific oceans and the Gulf of Mexico. The total coastline of the Great Lakes, including islands, is 11,000 miles (17,703 kilometers). The State of Michigan alone has 3,200 miles (5,150 km) of shoreline, which is more than any other state except Alaska.

Moving inland from the shoreline, several rivers and streams drain into the Great Lakes. The landmass that drains into these rivers and streams and into the Great Lakes is called the Great Lakes Basin. The Great Lakes Basin, commonly referred to as a watershed, covers about 295,000 square miles (764,046 sq. km) of land. Some of the larger rivers that drain into the lakes include the Saint Louis, Little Calumet, Saugeen, Cuyahoga, Grand, and Oswego.

FIRE AND ICE

The formation of the Great Lakes Basin, in which millions of people live and work today, took billions of years to complete. About

◄ *The coastline of the Great Lakes is so long that it has been nicknamed "The Fourth Coast." This is part of Lake Superior's shoreline.*

Some shoreline areas of Lake Superior bear the remains of ancient volcanic activity.

three billion years ago, volcanoes began erupting and spewed fiery lava over much of the area north and northwest of the Great Lakes. The dark cliffs that line Lake Superior's shores and the pitted rocks on many of that lake's beaches are reminders of those ancient volcanoes. Then earthquakes lifted up and folded the hardened lava to form mountains. Some remains of those ancient mountains are the flattened bedrock between the Great Lakes and Hudson Bay in Canada and the ridge that runs through the center of Isle Royale in the United States.

The mountains were worn down by the weight and motion of a shallow, warm, saltwater sea. From about 600 million to 245 million years ago this ocean washed over much of North America. During that time, what is now the Great Lakes region enjoyed a tropical climate. Corals, mollusks, trilobites, and other organisms lived in the warm water. When these animals died, they sank to the bottom of the sea and formed a thick limestone seabed. After the saltwater sea receded, it left a circle of shale in what is now the Great Lakes region. Rain and wind eroded the soft shale and formed an ancient riverbed that stretched through what are now the Great Lakes.

About two million years ago the last Ice Age began. Temperatures dropped, and more snow fell than melted. Over thousands of years, the unmelted snow piled up in layers, forming sheets of ice that were more than a mile (1.6 km) thick and several hundred miles wide. Eventually, these huge sheets of ice, which are called

Sandstone and shale formations can be found along the shore of Devils Island on Lake Superior.

glaciers, began to slide slowly south over the area that now contains the Great Lakes.

For more than one million years, glaciers advanced and retreated at least ten times over the area now known as the Great Lakes. After each retreat, or melting of a glacier, the temperatures increased, and the land that had been flattened by the glacier would rise about 1 foot (30 centimeters) every one hundred years. With each advance, the glaciers dug deep into the ancient riverbed, scouring out even deeper and wider depressions. Also during each advance, the glaciers pushed along huge amounts of soil and rock. This debris was left in place when the glaciers retreated. Some of the soil and rocks were deposited in the ancient riverbed, narrowing or blocking it. These narrows became the rivers and straits that connect the Great Lakes today. The weight and movement of the glaciers ground up other debris into sand, gravel, and clay, which formed the land along the Great Lakes.

THE FORMATION OF THE LAKES

From about 10,000 to 15,000 years ago, the last glacier in the Great Lakes region melted. The freshwater that was left behind began to fill in the deep depressions left by the glaciers. The southernmost depressions filled first, and the northernmost ones filled last. At first these glacial lakes were much larger than the present-day Great Lakes. For example, Lake Erie flowed west into what is now Lake Michigan, and Lake Michigan flowed into what is now the Chicago

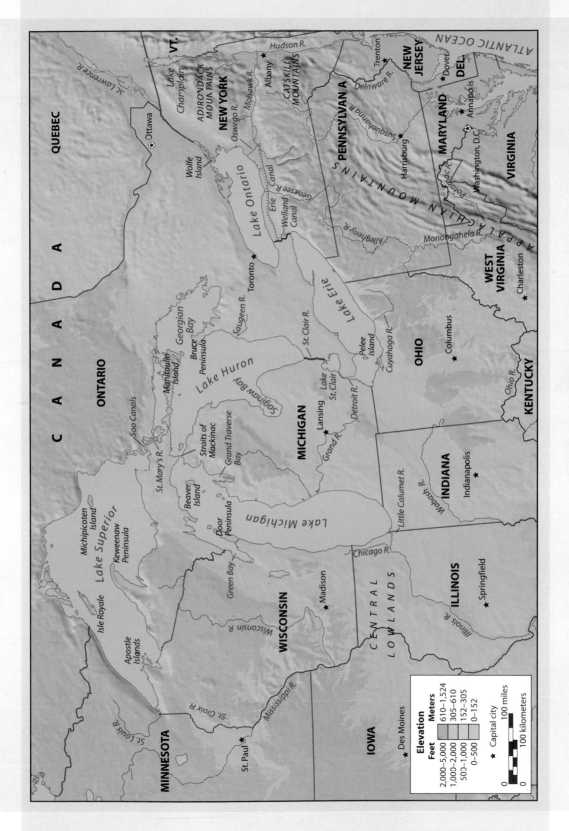

PHYSICAL MAP OF THE GREAT LAKES

River, then into the Illinois River and on to the Mississippi River.

The land around the early Great Lakes continued to rise about 1 foot (30 cm) every one hundred years. By about ten thousand years ago, the land surrounding the lakes had risen enough to stop the lakes from overflowing. Also by that time, the land had developed a tilt from southwest to northeast. In other words, the water from the Great Lakes flowed from Lake Michigan to Lake Ontario, then up the Saint Lawrence River to the Atlantic Ocean. At that time, Lake Erie reached its present level and became the first Great Lake to be

Connecting waters of the Niagara River carry water from Lake Erie over Niagara Falls.

completed. About three thousand years later, Lake Ontario reached its present level and began emptying into the Saint Lawrence River, just as it does today. Lakes Huron and Michigan reached their present levels, which are the same, about three thousand years ago. Lake Superior's present level was also reached about that same time.

As glacial ice melted, rivers also formed between the Great Lakes. These rivers are referred to as connecting waters. The Saint Mary's River linked Lake Superior to Lake Huron. The Saint Clair River, Lake Saint Clair, and the Detroit River connected Lake Huron to

Lake Erie. Water from Lake Erie traveled down the Niagara River, over Niagara Falls, into Lake Ontario, and eventually to the Atlantic Ocean through the Saint Lawrence River. The water in the Great Lakes follows this same route today.

UNIQUE QUALITIES OF EACH LAKE

Although the Great Lakes are sometimes thought of as a group, each lake has its own unique qualities. Lake Superior is the largest, deepest, highest, and coldest of the lakes. Lake Superior is also the youngest of the lakes—the last one to reach its present level. One might think that all those "-ests" are what gave the lake its name.

Solitary Loon Island is located in the North Channel of Lake Huron.

The Lakes by the Numbers

	SUPERIOR	HURON	MICHIGAN	ERIE	ONTARIO
Surface Water Area (square miles)	31,700	22,973	22,278	9,906	7,340
Maximum Length	350 miles	206 miles	307 miles	210 miles	193 miles
Maximum Width	160 miles	183 miles	118 miles	57 miles	53 miles
Maximum Depth	1,335 feet	748 feet	925 feet	210 feet	804 feet
Volume of Water	2,934 cu mi	850 cu mi	1,180 cu mi	116 cu mi	393 cu mi
Shoreline	2,726 miles	3,827 miles	1,659 miles	871 miles	726 miles
Elevation (all above sea level)	600 feet	579 feet	579 feet	570 feet	245 feet

French explorers named the lake "Superior" because it was higher in elevation than the other lakes. In French *supérieur* means "higher" or "upper." The shape of Lake Superior resembles the head of a wolf, with the tip of its nose at Duluth, Minnesota; Michigan's Isle Royale as an eye; and the Keweenaw Peninsula, also in Michigan, as its lower jaw. This symbol is fitting for the lake with the most wilderness area along its shores.

Named by the French after the Huron Indians who lived by its shore, Lake Huron was the first of the Great Lakes to be explored by Europeans. This lake has the longest shoreline and the largest island, Manitoulin, of the five lakes. Manitoulin Island and the

Chicago, with a population of more than 2.8 million people, grew along the shores of Lake Michigan.

Bruce Peninsula almost cut off Huron's Georgian Bay from the rest of the lake. Because of this, Lake Huron is sometimes thought of as two lakes. Both Lakes Huron and Michigan are at the same elevation above sea level. Because of this fact, the two lakes could be considered one. Also because they are at the same elevation above sea level, they do not need a river to connect them. Instead, they are linked by the Straits of Mackinac. The shores of Lake Huron have some of the Great Lakes' largest stretches of farmland, as well as the world's longest sandy beach along fresh water.

Lake Michigan's name comes from the Algonquin word *michigami*, which means "big water." This lake hangs like a sack between Lakes Superior and Huron and looks something like a salamander, with its head at the southern shore, and Green Bay and Grand Traverse Bay for legs. Of all the lakes, Michigan has the largest population living and working along its shores.

Named for the Erie Indians, Lake Erie is the shallowest of the lakes and holds the least water. Because of these characteristics Lake Erie was completely formed before the other Great Lakes. That makes Lake Erie the oldest of the lakes. More fish are caught in Lake Erie than in all the other Great Lakes combined. Like the other Great Lakes, Lake Erie supports industrial cities and farmland along its shores. Lake Erie is also known as the most dangerous of the lakes. Fierce windstorms blowing from west to east at speeds of up to 100 miles per hour (161 kph) can develop with no warning. These storms are believed to have caused more shipwrecks on Lake Erie than on the other Great Lakes.

Lake Ontario is the smallest of the lakes. Its name comes from an Iroquois word meaning "beautiful water." Canada's largest urban areas form a strip along the lake's northwest shore.

WATER, WIND, AND WAVES

The Great Lakes are dynamic, ever-changing, ever-moving bodies of water. Throughout the year, the Great Lakes lose about 1 percent of their water. Some of this loss is water that flows from lake to lake into the Saint Lawrence River. Another loss occurs when surface water on the lakes evaporates into the air and becomes water vapor. Still other losses occur when water is taken from the lakes and used for drinking, household purposes, farming, and industry. Much of the water that leaves the lakes each year is replaced by rainfall and snowfall; by drainage from rivers, creeks, and streams; by runoff from nearby land; and by groundwater.

Twice a year, in the spring and fall, the water in each lake does a somersault, or what scientists refer to as a turnover. This turnover is caused by a change in the temperature and density of the water. Dense water is heavy. When the temperature of surface water drops to 39 degrees Fahrenheit (4 degrees celsius) in the fall, the water is most dense and sinks to the bottom of the lake. At that point, warmer water rises to the surface and causes the turnover. This process is reversed when the surface water warms in the springtime. This turnover is an important ecological process that helps distribute oxygen and sustain aquatic life in the lakes. During the summer, the lakes' water forms layers based on temperature. The surface layer is warmed by the sun, has the most oxygen, and supports the most plant life. Water below 45 feet (13 meters) from the surface forms a cold layer because the sun's rays do not reach it. A middle layer between the warmest and coldest layers acts as a transfer zone, allowing the lakes' waters to continually mix. Then in the fall the surface water begins to lose its heat, and the cycle starts over again.

While not always predictable, the water levels of the lakes also follow regular cycles. Since scientists have been keeping records, they have observed that the lakes go through a thirty-year cycle in which water levels can change by as much as 6 inches (15 cm). Within this thirty-year cycle, the lakes' levels also may change by 1 or 2 feet (30 or 60 cm) twice each year. During the winter, the lakes are at their lowest levels because much of their water is tied up in ice, and there is no water runoff from land. Lake levels are highest in the summer, when all the snow and ice have melted, and the lakes receive water from rain and runoff.

During winter, lake levels drop as water becomes trapped in the solid ice.

Waves on the Great Lakes are different from ocean waves. They are more frequent, thus creating choppy waters.

Wind and waves can also temporarily change Lake levels in a matter of hours. A wave called a **seiche** (pronounced "saysh") is created by a quick change of wind and air pressure. *Seiche* is a French word that means "to sway back and forth." During a seiche, a large wave of water is pushed from the west end of a lake to the east end, causing the water to pile up on the eastern shore. When the wind stops, the water rushes back the other way and levels out again. Lake Erie experiences more seiches than the other Great Lake because of its west-east orientation and its shallow depth. In 1979 a storm seiche caused a water level difference of 14 feet (4 m) between Toledo and

Buffalo, cities on opposite ends of the lake. Sometimes seiches can be extremely dangerous and have even claimed human lives.

Waves on the Great Lakes can be more dangerous than those in oceans. Because the lakes are smaller than oceans, there is less distance between waves. This gives the lakes' waves a lot of chop. The waves come quickly, one after another, and chop on shores and toss boats and ships around.

LAKE EFFECT: SPECIAL WEATHER PATTERNS

During weather reports, people in the Great Lakes Basin are used to hearing "cooler by the lake" in the summer and "warmer by the lake" in the winter. Like all large bodies of water, the Great Lakes affect the climate of nearby land. Because the lakes absorb heat from the sun in the summer months, the land closest to them is cooler than the land farther from the lakes. That is why Duluth, Minnesota, on Lake Superior, advertises itself in summer as "The Air-Conditioned City." The lakes' surface water near the shore holds onto its heat until late fall/early winter. Winds blowing toward the shore cause temperatures to be higher near the lakes than those farther inland during that time of the year. Parts of southern Ontario, western New York, and much of Michigan experience warmer winter temperatures than states farther south but farther from the lakes.

In the fall, a clash of warm and cold air over the lakes can stir up severe storms. One storm that sailors on the lakes greatly fear is called the November Witch. This storm occurs in early to mid-November. It combines almost hurricane-force winds, high waves, low temperatures, and rain or sometimes snow. Many shipwrecks, including that of the *Edmund Fitzgerald*, have occurred during such a storm. In some November storms, waves on Lake Michigan have reached 20 to 25 feet (6 to 7 m) high. High waves have crossed Lake Shore Drive in Chicago. Spray from the waves has reached several stories high on apartment buildings.

Lake-effect snow is another Great Lakes weather phenomenon. In winter, when cold, dry air from the Arctic blows over the warmer water of the lakes, it picks up moisture. When this air reaches land, the moisture falls as several inches to a couple of feet of snow. At the same time, land only a few miles from the lakes might receive no snow at all. Lake-effect snow falls mainly on the eastern shores of the Great Lakes, as well as on the southeastern shores of Lake Superior and Lake Michigan.

Lake Erie is the only lake that regularly freezes over. This occurs because of the shallowness of that lake. Water on the other lakes freezes only near the shore.

LANDSCAPES ALONG THE LAKES

The geologic forces that shaped the Great Lakes also formed the land along the lakes, as well as islands in the lakes. The Great Lakes' islands make up the world's largest group of freshwater islands. Most of the islands contain their own lakes; some with

An autumn storm on Lake Superior ▷▷ sends waves pounding onto the North Shore in Minnesota.

The brown, tan, and green sandstone cliffs of Pictured Rocks National Lakeshore on Lake Superior were sculpted by wind, waves, and ice.

their own islands. In fact, Ryan Island is famous for being the largest island in the largest lake (Siskiwit Lake) on the largest island (Isle Royale) in the largest lake (Lake Superior).

Lake Superior's northern shore is protected by tall, dark cliffs of volcanic rock. In some places, the cliffs rise about 1,000 feet (305 m) above the water. Nearby are the Superior National Forest in Minnesota and the Pukaskwa National Park in Ontario, Canada. Isle Royale National Park, in Michigan, is in the northwestern part of Lake Superior. Much of the lake's southern shore is lined by multicolored sandstone bluffs, which make up Pictured Rocks National Lakeshore. Wind and water have carved strange shapes into these bluffs. The Apostle Islands National Lakeshore is also in this part of the lake. Close to Superior's southern shores are the Ottawa and Hiawatha national forests.

Lake Huron's northern shore has many rocky inlets. The northern part of the lake is also where most of Huron's 30,000 islands are located. Although most of the islands are small, Manitoulin Island, the world's largest freshwater island, is in Lake Huron. Along the Bruce Peninsula, many strange-looking limestone rock formations, such as Flower Pot Island, shoot up from the shore. They are part of Canada's Bruce Peninsula National Park. On the western shore, in Michigan, forests, including the Huron National Forest, still cover much of the land.

Lake Michigan's shores are known mainly for their wide, sandy beaches and high sand dunes. Winds blowing from the west pushed sand from the lake's eastern shore, forming dunes in various places. Today, these huge piles of sand are the largest network of freshwater dunes in the world. The wind continues to shape and move the dunes. At about 460 feet (140 m) high, Sleeping Bear Dunes toward the north of Lake Michigan are the world's highest sand dunes. They make up Sleeping Bear Dunes National Lakeshore, which covers 71,199 acres (28,813 hectares). At the southern end of Lake Michigan, Indiana Dunes National Lakeshore covers about 15,000 acres (6,070 ha). The lake's northwestern shores are better known for forested limestone bluffs. All of Lake Michigan's islands are in the northern part of the lake, the largest of which is Beaver Island, Michigan.

Lake Erie's shoreline is mostly flat land, much of which is used for farming. The lake's western end has many marshy wetlands and sandy beaches, as well as the lake's largest islands. Kelleys Island's

Glacial Grooves State Memorial has 15-foot (4.5-m) deep grooves about 100 feet (30 m) long that were carved into the limestone by glaciers thousands of years ago. Much of the lake's western end has high, rocky land.

Land along northern Lake Ontario is a broad plain, which is mainly used for farming. Along Ontario's southwestern shore are the remains of the shoreline from the ancient saltwater sea that once covered the land. Sandy beaches, rocky shores, and wetlands are also found along Lake Ontario.

Dunes as high as 180 feet (54 m) rise above Lake Michigan at the Indiana Dunes National Lakeshore.

THREE

Plants and Animals of the Great Lakes Region

In addition to shaping the land and influencing the climate, the Great Lakes also affect the region's plant and animal life in many ways. The communities of plants and animals in the region interacting with their natural environment makes up the Great Lakes' **ecosystem**. More than 3,500 species of plants and animals live in the Great Lakes Basin.

Within this ecosystem, four major habitats provide places where the plants and animals live: marshes and shoreline areas, dune formations, forests, and the lakes themselves, the largest of the habitats. Hundreds of aquatic plants, fish, and mollusks (clams, mussels, and snails) live in the Great Lakes. Along parts of the lakes' shores, grassy marshes provide another habitat for other fish, birds, and small mammals. Sand dunes have formed on other parts of the shores, providing places for grasses, shrubs, and trees to take root. Near other shores and a bit farther inland, forests with trees, flowers, and berries are home to other kinds of birds and larger mammals.

◄◄ *Moose can be found in the northern Great Lakes region.*

GREAT LAKES WETLANDS

Wetlands—marshes, swamps, fens, and bogs—are found along some shores and in some bays of the Great Lakes. Marshes and swamps lie mainly in the southern areas of the lakes; bogs and fens lie mainly in the north. Wetlands provide homes for fish, birds, and small animals. They also help filter out pollution before it can enter the lakes. Since the 1600s, the Great Lakes region has lost more than 66 percent of its natural wetlands. Farms, cities, industrial areas, and beaches have taken their place.

Small animals make their homes in the wetlands of the Great Lakes.

Sheldon Marsh is one of the last wetlands along southwestern Lake Erie. It is a refuge for about three hundred kinds of birds, including woodpeckers, cardinals, chickadees, brown thrashers, green herons, geese, and egrets. Among the cattails, painted turtles sit on partly submerged logs, and carp flop about in the shallow water. Farther west, another wetland has muskrats that build lodges with grasses and sedges. Marshes also make great homes for black, canvasback, and mallard ducks, as well as Canada

Painted turtles sun themselves on a log.

geese, cormorants, and great blue herons. Besides cattails, plants of the wetlands include such wildflowers as blue iris.

The northern tip of Lake Michigan's Door Peninsula has more northerly types of wetlands. They range from grassy marshes to tree-filled swamps to moss-covered bogs. At Peninsula Park White Cedar Forest State Natural Area, yellow lady's slippers bloom at the base of white cedar and black spruce trees. Herons, mergansers, and mallard ducks live in this marshy bog, as do several kinds of frogs. Willows, dogwood, and alder trees grow in the Mink River Estuary. Black-crowned night herons and Cooper's hawks are a few of the birds living there.

LIFE IN THE LAKES' DUNES

The glaciers left huge piles of sand along what finally became the shores of the Great Lakes. Since then, wind and water have continued to build, shape, and move them into dunes. The dunes are found mainly on the eastern and western shores of the lakes. However, the largest ones are found on the eastern shores because of the stronger prevailing winds that blow from the west.

One of the largest areas of dunes is on the eastern shore of Lake Michigan. Since 1966 it has been part of Indiana Dunes National Lakeshore. Many plants and animals live in this dune area. Marram grass

Herons live in the dunes of the Great Lakes.

grows toward the bottom of the dunes. These plants have 20-foot (6-m) or longer roots that hold the sand in place so that other grasses, such as bluestem; flowers such as hoary puccoon, wood lilies, and lavender; and shrubs, such as sand cherry and wild grape; can take root. Decayed material from these plants form soil in which such trees as black oaks, cottonwoods, and jack pines can grow. Softshell turtles and birds such as buffleheads, gulls, and herons are a few of the animals that live in the dunes. Many of these dunes are very fragile and are harmed by people who build homes close to the lakes.

The Father of Ecology

Henry Chandler Cowles (1869–1939) was a scientist who studied plants and taught about them at the University of Chicago. In the late 1890s, he began a study of plant life on the Indiana dunes. He observed that each type of plant prepared the area for a more complex type of plant starting with grasses and ending with trees. This process, known as ecological succession, also occurs in wetlands and forests. Cowles wrote about this idea in *The Ecological Relations of the Vegetation on the Sand Dunes of Lake Michigan* (1899). Ecological succession became the basic idea behind the science of ecology. That is why Cowles is called the father of ecology.

FOREST LIFE

The largest forests with the greatest variety of trees stand in the northern Great Lakes region. That is also where the region's national, state, and provincial forests are located. Trees in the northern forests range from willowy, whitepaper birch to tall, sturdy white pines. Other trees include aspen, balsam fir, cedar, hemlock, maple, oak, and spruce. Blueberries, wintergreen, Dutchman's-breeches, lady's slippers, violets, and mosses grow on the forests' floors.

Forests in the Great Lakes region are the habitat for a diverse selection of wildlife.

Eagles, hawks, and osprey make their nests in the highest trees. They swoop out over the Great Lakes, looking for fish. When they spot one, they dive in feet first, grabbing the fish with their talons. Some of the largest land animals in the forests include black bears, foxes, deer, moose, and wolves. Minks, rabbits, and squirrels are a few of the smaller animals.

In the forests on Isle Royale in northwestern Lake Superior, the longest-running mammalian predator-prey study on earth is taking place. In 1959 scientists began studying the relationship between wolves (predators) and moose (prey) on the island. The island's isolation and the small number of other animals on the island make Isle Royale a great place to study the population changes caused by this predator-prey interaction. In addition, scientists study the relationship between the moose population and the condition of the balsam forests. Balsam fir is a favorite food of moose, and these trees grow in several areas of Isle Royale.

The black bear is one of the largest forest animals in the Great Lakes region.

LIFE IN THE LAKES

Aquatic plants, plants that live underwater or on the water's surface, are an important part of the Great Lakes ecosystem. They most often grow in the shallow areas near shore, including near islands. The plants provide food and shelter for fish, mollusks, waterbirds, and water insects. There are usually more fish in areas with abundant plant life. That is why many fishers like to fish "in the weeds." The root systems of aquatic plants also help hold the sand and soil near the shore in place. As with all green plants, aquatic plants release oxygen into the water through the process of photosynthesis.

Phytoplankton are small, microscopic plants that live in the lakes. Algae, diatoms, and duckweed are common examples of phytoplankton. These waterplants grow on submerged logs or rocks. They also float in clumps on top of lake water. In fact, Green Bay in Lake Michigan got its name from the huge mats of green algae that covered it. In addition, rooted aquatic plants can range from 3 to 12 feet (1 to 3.6 m) long. Some of the most common ones in the Great Lakes include bladderwort, common naiad, coon-

Algae and rooted aquatic plants are important features of the Great Lakes ecosystem.

Food chain in the Great Lakes

tail, muskgrass, quillwort, water milfoil, waterweed, and wild celery. Several kinds of pondweed—including clasping-leaf, curly, fern, and narrow-leaf—also grow in the Great Lakes. Pondweeds are an important source of food for waterfowl, such as American coots and mallard ducks.

Zooplankton are microscopic animals that live in and float on the lakes. They feed on the phytoplankton and in turn are eaten by insects, small fish, turtles, and waterfowl. Several kinds of insects grow and live in the Great Lakes, such as water bugs, water beetles, water scorpions, caddis flies, mayflies, and midges. Mayflies are

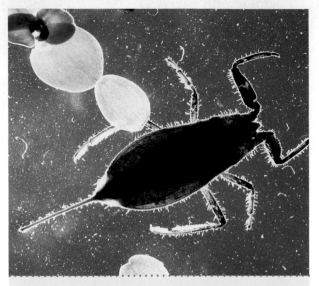
Water scorpions are found in the Great Lakes.

an especially important source of food for Great Lakes fish. They are also sensitive to pollution. In the mid-1900s, Lake Erie was heavily polluted, and most of the mayfly population disappeared. In the 1990s, mayflies reemerged in parts of Lake Erie and provided a sure sign that the lake's water quality was improving.

More than two hundred species of fish swim in the Great Lakes, from tiny smelt to 70-pound (32-kilogram) muskellunge and up to 300-pound (136-kg) lake sturgeon. Many of these fish are found in all the lakes, such as American eel, brook trout, carp, chub, northern pike, rainbow smelt, rainbow trout, salmon, sauger, shiner, sturgeon, silver lamprey, stickleback, trout perch, walleye, whitefish, and yellow perch. However, some fish are found in only one of the Great Lakes. For example, brook trout, bowfin, paddlefish, and yellow bullhead live in Lake Erie; tessellated darter, in Lake Ontario; chestnut lamprey and skipjack herring, in Lake Michigan; and pygmy whitefish and siscowet, in Lake Superior. Lake Erie has the greatest variety and amount of fish because it is the warmest and shallowest of the lakes. Lake Superior has the least variety and amount of fish because it is the coldest and deepest of the lakes.

FROM EXTINCT TO EXOTIC SPECIES

Throughout history, many animal species once found in the Great Lakes region have become extinct. At one time, prehistoric woolly mammoths, mastodons, saber-toothed tigers, and 500-pound (227 kg) beavers were plentiful in the Great Lakes Basin. As the climate and vegetation changed and prehistoric people hunted them, they disappeared. Recently, some Great Lakes animal species, such as the gray wolf and caribou, were endangered or threatened with extinction. Through various conservation and protection programs and new government policies, these animal populations have rebounded in some cases. However, several kinds of fish have become extinct throughout the lakes, including blackfin cisco, deepwater cisco, longjaw cisco, shortnose cisco, Ontario kiyi, blue pike, and spoonhead sculpin. All of the ciscos and the blue pike no longer exist at all on earth. The deepwater sculpin had become extinct in Lake Ontario but then

Gray wolves are no longer on the threatened and endangered species list in the Western Great Lakes region.

made a comeback. Overharvesting by commercial fishers and loss of habitat are the primary reasons that these species became extinct.

Since the 1800s, many new plant and animal species from around the globe have been introduced into the Great Lakes. These organisms are referred to as invasive or **exotic species**. Some of these species were intentionally introduced, such as the Pacific salmon, to help create a valuable fishery in the lakes. Others, such as the zebra mussel, were accidentally introduced and are having a negative impact on the lakes. The federal government and governments of the Great Lakes' states have passed laws to stop, or at least to limit, the unintentional introduction of exotic species. However, these laws have largely failed. Today, about 170 exotic species are found in the Great Lakes.

Chladophora, a quickly spreading algae, purple loosestrife, and Eurasian water milfoil are the main exotic plant species in the Great Lakes region. Purple loosestrife, an ornamental plant used in landscaping, has spread to wetlands near the lakes. There, it chokes off water from the native plants. Many birds that once ate or nested in these native plants have left the Great Lakes region. In an attempt to stop the spread of purple loosestrife, it has been declared illegal to sell this plant in many areas. Eurasian water milfoil multiples quickly into huge beds that choke off large areas of water to fish, small animals, boaters, and swimmers.

Among the more numerous exotic animal species are alewives, Asian carp, gobies, ruffs, sea lamprey, and zebra mussels. These

These zebra mussels were taken from Lake Erie. They raise problems that threaten the ecosystem of the lakes.

species come from all parts of the world. They arrived in the Great Lakes in a variety of ways, including swimming up the Saint Lawrence River or through canals, being released in ships' **ballast** water, and clinging to the side of ships and then releasing themselves. Because these animals have no natural enemies or predators in the lakes, they cause problems. For example, alewives eat a lot of zooplankton. With less zooplankton to eat phytoplankton or algae, parts of the lakes became choked with algae. Zebra mussels are named for their striped shells. One female zebra mussel can lay up to one million eggs per year. These mussels mature into adults in one year and can live about three years in the lakes. They are a problem because they eat much of the food (plankton and zooplankton) that would otherwise be available for fish to eat. Zebra mussels also clog the intake pipes of water utility companies along the lakes. These companies spend millions of dollars unclogging these water-intake lines.

Other nonnative fish have been introduced on purpose into the lakes. In the 1960s, chinook salmon and coho salmon from the Pacific Ocean were released into the lakes to control the alewife population. As a result, Alewives were dying in great numbers and washing up on beaches. The salmon were also used to encourage sport fishing. The lakes were also stocked with brown trout and rainbow trout for sport fishing.

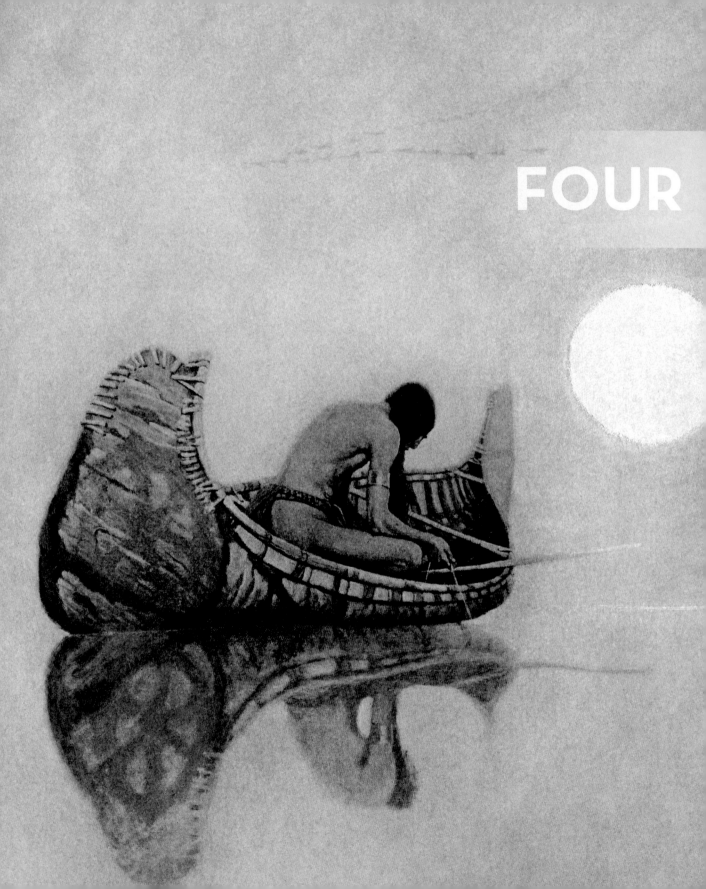

FOUR

The Inland Seas

People have been living in the Great Lakes region for at least ten thousand years. Called Paleo-Indians, these people hunted caribou, musk ox, and woolly mammoths. From the time that the first people entered the Great Lakes area, the lakes have been used for transportation and trade. By six thousand years ago, early people had discovered copper on Michigan's Upper Peninsula along Lake Superior. Pieces of fishhooks, harpoons, and knives made from this copper have been found as far east as New York. This shows that long-distance trade was taking place even at that time.

NATIVE AMERICANS

By the 1400s, people who are ancestors of today's Native Americans were living in the Great Lakes region. In Canada, Native Americans are known as First Nation People. The Tionontati and five Iroquois nations (Cayuga, Mohawk, Oneida, Onondaga, and Seneca) lived near Lake Ontario. The Iroquois nations formed a confederacy to fight common enemies. Some of the groups that the Iroquois fought were the Erie and Neutral near Lake Erie and the Huron from the

Many Native Americans have made the Great Lakes region their home for ten thousand years.

Lake Huron area. By the late 1600s, the Iroquois had defeated these other groups, who then moved farther west. The Native Americans living near Lakes Ontario, Erie, and Huron built homes called long-houses. These dwellings were framed with long, bent branches and were covered with bark. The Native Americans hunted deer, fished in the lakes with spears and nets, and grew crops of beans, corn, and squash.

Native Americans living near Lake Michigan included the Fox, Illinois, Kickapoo, Menominee, Miami, Potawatomi, and Winnebago. The main Native-American group living near Lake Superior was the Ojibwa, also called the Chippewa. These peoples lived in dome-shaped houses called wigwams. They hunted and fished, gathered wild rice from lakes, and tapped maple trees for sap to make sugar. The Ojibwa were known for the snowshoes and toboggans they crafted for traveling over snow.

EUROPEAN EXPLORERS AND TRADERS

By the early 1600s, about 117,000 Native Americans were living in the Great Lakes region. Between the early 1500s and the early 1600s, Europeans hoped to find a water route through North America to Asia to speed up the spice trade. In 1535 the French explorer Jacques Cartier sailed up the Saint Lawrence River and claimed all land to the west of it for France. He reached no farther than what is now the city of Montreal, Quebec, in Canada. The French began trading European goods with the nearby Native Americans for furs. The first European officially to see the Great Lakes was the French explorer Samuel de Champlain. In 1615 he reached Georgian Bay in Lake Huron. Champlain and his men paddled canoes from Quebec up the Ottawa River, **portaged** across land to Lake Nipissing, and canoed down the French River to Lake Huron. Champlain had hoped that Lake Huron was a saltwater sea that would lead him to Asia.

Étienne Brûlé was probably the first European to see four of the Great Lakes. In 1610 Champlain sent Brûlé to live with the Algonquin and learn their language. Brûlé is believed to have reached Lake Huron at that time and to have reached

An early explorer to the Great Lakes region was Jacques Cartier, who is credited with discovering the Saint Lawrence River.

Lakes Ontario and Erie in 1615. Champlain also sent Brûlé farther west, where he came upon Lake Superior in 1622. The first European to arrive in Lake Michigan was Jean Nicolet. Again, Champlain sent him there, in 1634. Nicolet landed in Green Bay dressed in lavish Chinese robes. He thought he would be arriving in Asia. Instead, he was greeted by the Winnebago.

Later in the 1600s, other Frenchmen sailed farther around the lakes. Médard Chouart des Groseilliers, and Pierre Esprit Radisson explored Lake Superior in 1659 and 1660. Later in 1669, René-Robert Cavelier, Sieur de La Salle, explored Lake Ontario. In 1679 La Salle built and launched *Le Griffon*—the Great Lakes' first ship with sails. He sailed from Lake Erie and arrived in Green Bay on Lake Michigan later that year. La Salle sent his ship, loaded with furs, back east, but it sank either in Lake Michigan or Lake Huron. From Green Bay, La Salle went by canoe to the south end of Lake Michigan, becoming the first European to explore that lake.

Although the Great Lakes did not affect the rich Asian spice trade, they did open an even richer fur trade. Europeans wanted beaver fur hats, which held their shape and repelled rain and snow. From the 1600s to the early 1800s, the French and then the English carried on a brisk trade in furs with the Native Americans. Each spring voyageurs in Montreal filled long canoes with packs of wool blankets, metal pots, knives, and guns. They followed the same route that Champlain had taken in 1615. From Lake Huron, they paddled to the Saint Mary's River, portaged to Lake Superior, and canoed along the north shore of Lake Superior to Fort William in Ontario or to Grand Portage, near the Minnesota-Ontario border. The trip took eight weeks. At the fort or Grand Portage, they exchanged their goods for bundles of beaver fur gathered by French traders who traded with Native Americans to the west. The voyageurs headed back the same way, arriving in Montreal before the fall storms hit the lakes.

Along the lakes, the French built other trading posts. French

Catholic missionaries also traveled along the lakes and built missions for their work in converting the Native Americans to Christianity. In the mid- to late-1600s, Jesuit priests set up missions at Sault Sainte Marie and Saint Ignace, near Ashland, Wisconsin, and on Green Bay. In 1670 the French began building forts on the Great Lakes to protect the fur traders and the missions.

When the British arrived in North America, they set up colonies along the Atlantic Ocean. Eventually, they came into conflict with the French over control of the land to the west and of the fur trade. Between 1754 and 1763, the French and British fought the French and Indian War. This war got its name because several Native-American tribes sided with the French. The British won the war, and the French were forced to leave Canada. This left the British in control of the Great Lakes and the fur trade.

French traders paddled along rivers to trade their goods with the Native Americans in the Great Lakes region.

TWO NEW COUNTRIES ON THE GREAT LAKES

By 1775 many people in the British colonies thought of themselves as Americans. They wanted to be independent of Great Britain and began the Revolutionary War (1775–1783). Some colonists who remained loyal to Britain fled to the Lake Ontario region of Canada. In 1783 the Americans had won their independence and had gained all of Britain's land east of the Mississippi River. As part of the peace treaty, what is now the U.S.–Canada boundary line was drawn through the Great Lakes.

The War of 1812, between Great Britain and the United States, lasted until 1815. Among other things, Britain hoped to regain control of the Great Lakes. In 1813 American ships under the control of Oliver Hazard Perry defeated the British in the Battle of Lake Erie near Put-in-Bay. This victory ensured U.S. control over the southern part of the Great Lakes.

By the 1830s, people in the Canadian provinces began seeking self-government. In 1867, Britain united the provinces as the Dominion of Canada. Ottawa, of the dominion in the Great Lakes province of Ontario, became the capital.

SHIPPING, CANALS, PORTS, AND BRIDGES

Since the mid-1700s, Americans, Canadians, and the British used sailing ships to carry goods back and forth on the Great Lakes. Lake schooners with sails specially designed for Great Lakes winds and waves plied the lakes into the early 1900s. Steam-powered ships arrived on the Great Lakes in 1816 with the launch of the *Frontenac* on Lake Ontario near Kingston, Ontario. One of the first American steamships on the lakes was the *Walk-in-the-Water*, launched on Lake Erie in 1818. It made several trips between Buffalo, New York, and Detroit, Michigan, and into Green Bay before running aground near Buffalo in an November 1821 storm. Besides cargo, the steamships also carried passengers. These ships did not depend on wind to propel them and therefore could keep to more regular schedules than boats with sails.

Ships had no problem sailing between Lake Erie and Lake Huron because there was a gradual change in elevation of about 8 feet (2 m), with no waterfalls between the two. The ships simply went up the Detroit River, into Lake Saint Clair, then up the Saint Clair River. Likewise, ships traveled easily between Lake Huron and Lake Michigan through the Straits of Mackinac, because the two lakes have the same elevation. However, the drop in elevation of 326 feet (99 m) between Lake Erie and Lake Ontario over Niagara Falls prevented ships from traveling between these lakes. The same was true for the 23-foot (7-m) drop over the Sault Sainte Marie (the falls of the Saint Mary's River) between Lake Superior and Lake Huron. To solve these problems, Canada and the United States dug canals. The canals had several sets of locks, which are boxlike steps that fill with water to raise and lower ships as they travel from one water level to

Grain barges are towed north from Chicago on Lake Michigan.

another. In Canada, the Welland Canal, completed in 1829, linked Lakes Ontario and Erie by avoiding Niagara Falls. In 1855 and 1895, the Soo Canals were completed at Sault Sainte Marie. Finally, the five Great Lakes were linked.

With the linking of the lakes, trade increased on these inland waterways. In addition, great numbers of people from the northeastern United States, as well as from many European countries, traveled on the lakes to reach and settle on land in the Great Lakes basin. Towns with ports or harbors grew into cities, such as Buffalo, New York; Cleveland, Ohio; Detroit, Michigan; Chicago, Illinois; Milwaukee,

Wisconsin; and Duluth, Minnesota. On the Canadian side, Kingston, Toronto, Hamilton, Sarnia, Sault Sainte Marie, and Port Arthur (now called Thunder Bay) developed as port cities. Today, the Port of the Duluth-Superior is the busiest Great Lakes port, handling more than 44 million tons (40 million m tons) of cargo each year.

Since their completion, the Welland and Soo canals have been deepened and widened several times to hold increasingly larger ships. By the mid-1900s, steamships on the Great Lakes had given way to diesel-powered freighters. In 1959 the Great Lakes were opened to oceangoing vessels to expand international trade in the

The Sault Sainte Marie Canal connected Lakes Superior and Huron.

Great Lakes region. In that year, the first ships entered the Saint Lawrence Seaway from the Atlantic Ocean. The building of the seaway took five years and was a joint project of the U.S. and Canadian governments. Canals and locks were built to avoid rapids and falls on the Saint Lawrence River. To accommodate oceangoing vessels, connections between the lakes were deepened. They included the Detroit River, Lake Saint Clair, the Saint Clair River, and the Straits of Mackinac. The Welland and Soo canals were also improved. In addition, Great Lakes ports and harbors were deepened.

While canals linked the lakes, bridges linked land across the lakes. With the coming of the railroads by the mid-1800s and the manufacture of automobiles and the building of highways in the early 1900s, the Great Lakes needed bridges. One of the most famous bridges on the lakes is the Aerial Lift Bridge at the Port of Duluth. Built in 1930, this drawbridge lifts straight up to allow large ships into the port. The longest bridge on the lakes is the Mackinac Straits Bridge, with a main span of 3,800 feet (1,158 m). Built in 1957, it connects Michigan's Upper and Lower peninsulas. On the eastern edge of the Lower Peninsula, the 1,850-foot (563-m) Ambassador Bridge, built in 1929, connects Detroit, Michigan, to Windsor, Ontario.

The city of Buffalo, New York, grew and thrived along the shore of Lake Erie.

CARGO ON THE GREAT LAKES

Since the 1600s, many types of goods have been shipped on the Great Lakes. In the early 1800s, the fur trade ended because there were few beavers left in the northern forests. Also, beaver hats had gone out of fashion. Lumber quickly replaced the fur. The forests of northern Michigan, Wisconsin, and Minnesota were full of tall, straight, white pine trees. Lumber from these trees was sought after for building ships, homes, and other structures in the Great Lakes area. The trees were cut down, and the logs were floated down rivers to the Great Lakes. There they were loaded onto schooners or steamships and taken to shipyards and ports in the growing Great Lakes cities. In the early 1900s, the lumber trade had leveled off. Most of the pine forests, as well as other forests, had been chopped down, and other building products, such as bricks and steel, were replacing wood.

In the mid-1800s, copper and iron ore mining had become important industries on Michigan's Upper Peninsula. In the late 1800s, huge deposits of iron ore were found in northern Minnesota. By this time, several railroads ran through the Great Lakes region. Railroad cars carried the ore from the mines to Lake Superior ports. From there, the ore was shipped to other Great Lakes ports that had large iron forges. Later, the ore was used to make steel in giant mills along the lakes, from Chicago to Erie, Pennsylvania. Coal was needed to heat the iron in the forges and mills. This resource was sent by train from West Virginia, southern Pennsylvania, and southern

Illinois to the Great Lakes and then by ship to the forges and mills. Ships going back up the lakes often carried limestone used in buildings.

Many families that had settled in the Great Lakes region of both Canada and the United States, as well as in areas farther west, were made up of farmers. Some farmers grew huge cash crops of wheat, corn, and other grains, which they sold to food processors. At first, railroads carried wheat and corn from Illinois and Wisconsin to eastern cities. Later, these crops came from western Minnesota and

The Christmas Tree Ship

Each November, a lumber schooner called the *Rouse Simmons* made one last trip down Lake Michigan from Manistique, Michigan, to Chicago. Its cargo on that trip was blue spruce trees sold as Christmas trees. At the dock on the Chicago River the ship's captain sold the trees either for $.50 cents to $1 or gave them away to poor families. In November 1912, the *Rouse Simmons* did not make it to Chicago. A severe storm battered the ship until it sank, along with its crew, near Two Rivers, Wisconsin. Since then, the *Rouse Simmons* has been known as "The Christmas Tree Ship." Songs and a play have been written about it. The play is produced in a Chicago-area theater during the Christmas season.

A freighter heavy with cargo approaches Detroit, Michigan.

the Dakotas to the Port of Duluth and from western Canada into Port Arthur. From there, they were shipped to eastern cities and processed into flour. Livestock, such as hogs, dairy products, and processed meats were also shipped along the inland seas.

Eventually, competition from railroads and trucks on highways cut into shipping on the Great Lakes. Today, however, the main cargoes on the Great Lakes are still grain, iron ore, and coal. It is often cheaper to transport these items by water than to carry them overland on railroads or in trucks on highways.

THE FISHING INDUSTRY

The commercial fishing industry on the lakes started in about 1820. By the mid-1800s, fishing had become a major commercial industry on Lake Superior. By 1889, about 147 million pounds (66 million kg) of fish were caught each year in the five lakes. Little by little the catches of favorite fish dwindled and then gave out. On Lake Superior, the whitefish went first, so fishers turned to lake trout. When the trout gave out, fishers turned to lake herring. The same thing happened on the other lakes. Smaller, less valuable fish replaced the larger, more valuable, and more popular fish. By the 1950s the Great Lakes fishing industry had seen its best years come and go.

Today, the Canadian fishing industry is still doing well, with fairly large catches of perch and walleye from Lake Erie. In the United States, most of the commercial catches are lake whitefish. Alewives are caught and used for animal feed. Sport fishing groups would like to see less commercial fishing so more fish would be available for their leisure sport.

SHIPS, LIGHTHOUSES, AND SAFETY

Estimates range from six thousand to ten thousand for the number of ships that have sunk in the Great Lakes since about 1800. With those ships, about 30,000 crew members lost their lives. Many of those shipwrecks were caused by storms that developed quickly with no warning, by ships running into each other, and by fires. However, other ships hit rocks or ran aground because crews could not see the tips of peninsulas or other land.

Today, 312 lighthouses stand along the Great Lakes' 11,000-mile (17,703-km) coastlines. In 1804, the British built the first lighthouse on the Great Lakes on Lake Ontario. It remained standing until 1814. In 1808, Gibraltar Point Light was built in Toronto on Lake Ontario. Today, it is the oldest lighthouse on the lakes; however, its light is no longer lit. On the American side of the lakes the first lights were lit in 1819 on Lake Erie at Buffalo, New York, and Erie, Pennsylvania. Like the Gibraltar Point Light, many Great Lakes lights are no longer lit. Those that still function turn on and off automatically, with no need for a lighthouse keeper. Some Great Lakes lighthouses are open to

Split Rock Lighthouse was built in the early 1900s because of increased iron ore shipments on Lake Superior.

the public as museums. Split Rock Light on Lake Superior is the most visited of these lighthouses.

Now ship captains rely on radar, sonar, and global positioning satellites (GPS) to guide them on their way. Even these aids can fail, as happened when the *Edmund Fitzgerald* went down in a storm on Lake Superior in 1975. In general, however, traveling on the Great Lakes in the twenty-first century is much safer than it was in the past. Ships are built better and stronger. Their seams are welded and no longer riveted together. Also, there are more government controls and laws to ensure that captains and lead crew members are trained and licensed.

FIVE

An Inland Megalopolis

When flying at night from upstate New York to Milwaukee, Wisconsin, passengers looking out their windows can see an almost continuous ribbon of lights. The lights are from the office buildings and homes in the cities, suburbs, and towns that line the shores of the Great Lakes. Canada's northern shore of Lake Ontario has a similar line of cities and suburbs. This unending stretch of communities is called a **megalopolis**, or a giant-size city.

People have been attracted to the Great Lakes region since the end of the Ice Age for many reasons. First, the lakes' clear, freshwater was good for drinking and cooking. Second, the lakes themselves contained fish for food. Third, the fish attracted ducks, geese, and mammals. In turn, people hunted those animals. Fourth, the lakes provided a transportation route through the region that allowed people and goods to move faster than they would overland. Today, most of these reasons still hold true, only on a larger scale. Cities and suburbs of the megalopolis need lake water for homes and industries. Nearby farms need lake water to irrigate the fields. Hydroelectric and nuclear power plants need lake water to produce electricity. In addition, people now use the lakes for recreation and leisure activities.

THE PEOPLE OF THE GREAT LAKES REGION

When the first Europeans arrived, about 117,000 Native Americans were living in the Great Lakes region. Today, four hundred years later, about forty-two million people live in this region, which includes the United States and Canada. They make up about 30 percent of Canada's population and a bit more than 10 percent of the population of the United States. Toronto on Lake Ontario is Canada's largest city and the largest city on Lake Ontario. Chicago (on Lake

The largest city in the Great Lakes region is Chicago, Illinois.

A high school marching band wears wooden shoes in Holland, Michigan, during the Tulip Festival.

Michigan) is the third-largest U.S. city and the largest of all the cities in the Great Lakes region.

Of course, not everyone in the Great Lakes region lives in cities. Some live in small towns and on farms. Many kinds of crops are grown and animals are raised on farms in the Great Lakes region. Some farms also have grape vineyards and orchards of fruit trees, such as apple and cherry trees. These fruits grow especially well in the climates created by the lakes.

The people who live in Great Lakes' cities or on farms nearby can trace their heritages to just about every country in the world. Milwaukee is known for its German population; Chicago for its Irish. Toledo has a large Lebanese population. Buffalo and Cleveland have large Polish populations. Holland, Michigan, settled by Dutch people, still celebrates its heritage with an annual Tulip Festival. Northern Minnesota, Wisconsin, and Michigan have large populations with

Native Americans celebrate their culture and heritage during an annual powwow.

Swedish, Norwegian, and Finnish backgrounds. By the mid-1900s, great numbers of African Americans had moved from southern states to Great Lakes cities to find manufacturing jobs, primarily in the automobile industry. During the late 1900s and into the early 2000s, immigrants from China, Korea, and India found work in these cities and their suburbs. Others came from Russia and other former Soviet states to make a better life in the Great Lakes region. Refugees from civil wars in Africa also have made their homes in Great Lakes cities. Hispanic people from Mexico and countries in

South America have also moved to the Great Lakes cities to find jobs and a better way of life.

NATIVE AMERICANS IN THE GREAT LAKES REGION

A great number of Native Americans and First Nation people still live in the Great Lakes area. The largest group is the Ojibwa. Members of the Menominee, Winnebago, Potawatomi, and Ottawa tribes also continue to live in the Great Lakes Basin. Many of them live on reservations, where the U.S. and Canadian governments moved them during the 1800s. This was done to make room for European settlers. Ontario's reservations are located mainly near the shores of Lake Superior and Lake Huron. Most of the reservations on the U.S. side of the Great Lakes are in northern Minnesota, Wisconsin, and Michigan. Some Native Americans living on these reservations earn their livelihoods by working in factories and shops or by harvesting wild rice. Some reservations also have resorts and casinos that attract tourists.

Many Native Americans continue to practice traditional ways of life. They use bows and arrows to hunt and spears and nets to fish. By setting nets across channels in the lakes, they can catch greater numbers of fish. This has caused problems with sport fishermen, who are allowed to catch only a certain number of each kind of fish. However, the Native-American groups have agreements with the U.S. government granting them special hunting and fishing rights.

CULTURE ALONG THE LAKES

Whenever great numbers of people settle in cities and towns, they soon build educational, sports, and cultural institutions, such as museums. From the University of Toronto to the State University of New York at Buffalo to the University of Minnesota, Duluth, the Great Lakes are home to some of the best universities in Canada and the United States. Just in the Chicago area alone, Loyola University, Northwestern University, and the University of Chicago are close to Lake Michigan.

Toronto, Buffalo, Cleveland, Detroit, Chicago, and Milwaukee are all great sports towns. Stiff lake winds often howl at NFL football games played at Cleveland Browns Stadium on the Lake Erie shore and at Chicago's Soldier Field on Lake Michigan's shore. The Toronto Blue Jays play Major League Baseball within an enclosed stadium close to Lake Ontario.

Two of the tallest buildings in the world provide landmarks along the lakes. CN Tower in Toronto, at 1,815 feet (553 m), is the world's tallest freestanding tower. Chicago has six of the world's fifty tallest buildings. Sears Tower at 110 stories and 1,450 feet (441 m), is the tallest building with occupied floors. The force of lake winds can be felt in both of these buildings.

Several museums also act as landmarks along the lakes. Cleveland's Rock and Roll Hall of Fame and Museum and the Great Lakes Science Center are neighbors to the football stadium. Environmental problems and solutions are displayed at the Science Center. The Adler Planetarium and Shedd Aquarium hug the lakeshore in Chicago. The Milwaukee Art Museum, with its winglike canopy that folds open on sunny days, juts out over Lake Michigan.

The tallest building along the shore of Lake Ontario in Canada is Toronto's CN Tower.

The Milwaukee Art Museum attracts visitors with its moveable winglike screen.

Smaller museums are also found along the lakes. In Duluth the Great Lakes Aquarium is devoted solely to the fish of the Great Lakes. Docked nearby is the *William A. Irvin*, a retired iron-ore and coal freighter, which can be toured for a glimpse of what it was ike to be working on the Great Lakes. The Great Lakes Shipwreck Museum on Whitefish Point, Michigan, is the only museum dedicated solely to telling the stories of the men and ships that have been lost on the Great Lakes. Although not a museum, the Mariners' Church of Detroit, near the Detroit River, has had its bell rung for each life lost whenever a ship has gone down on the lakes.

The Lakes in Poems, Songs, and Sculptures

Since the 1800s the Great Lakes have been cited in poems, songs, and sculptures. *The Song of Hiawatha*, the famous 1855 poem by Henry Wadsworth Longfellow, is based on an Ojibwa legend about a brave youth on Gitche Gumee. That was the Ojibwa name for Lake Superior.

In 1913, Lorado Taft, a famous Chicago sculptor, finished *Fountain of the Great Lakes*. Five female figures holding shells are grouped together like the five lakes. Water spills from their shells in the same way it flows down the lakes. Today, the fountain is at the Art Institute of Chicago.

Many songs have been written and sung based on the shipwrecks, storms, and the lives of sailors on the Great Lakes. Perhaps the most famous of these songs is "The Wreck of the Edmund Fitzgerald," written by Gordon Lightfoot in 1976. It tells the story of the last voyage of the "Mighty Fitz," as it was nicknamed. The freighter had picked up 26,000 tons (24,000 m tons) of iron ore at Superior, Wisconsin, and was on its way to Detroit, Michigan, to unload. It then was to go to Cleveland to dock for the winter months, when it got caught in a November Witch storm. It is believed that 30-foot (10-m) waves rolled the *Fitz* over on November 10, 1975, taking the crew of twenty-nine and Captain Ernest McSorley to the bottom of Lake Superior, off Whitefish Point, in Canadian waters.

RECREATION AT THE LAKES

The Great Lakes are a major recreational area for people living nearby and for tourists from other parts of Canada and the United States. A special activity is to **circumnavigate**—go completely around—the lakes. Some people follow highways that stay close to the shores. More adventurous travelers canoe, kayak, or sail close to the shoreline of the lakes. Every year, more than four million boats are launched on the lakes. They include various sizes of sailboats, speedboats, boats for sport fishing, and luxurious yachts. Many boaters keep their boats at docks or anchored in harbors in Great Lakes marinas. More than five million people fish on the lakes each year. Some fish from piers for perch and smelt. Some go out into deeper water to fish for bass and walleye.

The Fathom Five National Marine Park of Canada is an underwater national park in Lake Huron. Its crystal-clear waters reveal shipwrecks and sea life.

The lakes' public beaches attract several million people each summer. Wasaga Beach along northern Lake Huron is the world's longest freshwater beach. Beachcombers walk along the beaches looking for special rocks, shells, and other treasures. Except for Lake Superior, the lakes' shoreline summer water temperatures are usually warm enough for swimmers. However, scuba divers love exploring Lake Superior's clear, deep waters, with their many ship-wrecks and unusual underwater rock formations. Surfboarding, bodysurfing, and windsurfing are also popular activities on the lakes. The winds and waves on the Great Lakes are perfect for these sports. Most surfers wear wet suits to protect themselves from extreme winds and temperatures.

Some of the Great Lakes' visitors spend a day on the lake or at the beach and then go home. Others have second homes along the lakes or stay at resort hotels or cottages that have been built close to the lakes. A famous resort area of the Great Lakes is Mackinac (pronounced "MAH-kih-naw") Island, a part of Michigan that is in Lake Huron. The only ways to get to the island are by ferry or by plane. Once on Mackinac Island the only ways to get around are by walking, biking, or taking a horse-drawn carriage. Cars were banned from the island in 1898 to promote tourism—and it worked. Every summer, most hotels and cottages on the island are booked, especially at the popular Grand Hotel. Every summer the longest freshwater sailing race is run between Chicago and Mackinac Island. The boats are sailing yachts but can use only wind power during the race. The following weekend another race starts at Port Huron and ends at Mackinac Island.

Protecting the Lakes

From the mid-1800s to the 1960s, the Great Lakes were not treated as the great natural resource that they are. People acted as if the water of the lakes would last forever. They evidently did not realize that controls were needed to protect both the quality and the quantity of the water, as well as the ecology of shorelines.

WATER QUALITY

Since American and European settlers arrived in the Great Lakes Basin, they used the lakes for their drinking water. They also used them purposely or accidentally as dumping grounds for city sewage, industrial waste from mills and factories, and agricultural waste from farms. Although fertilizer from farms did not always go directly into a lake, it filtered down to groundwater supplies that eventually fed into the lakes.

Until 1900, the city of Chicago's sewage went directly into the Chicago River that in turn drained into Lake Michigan. From the 1850s, the city had experienced epidemics of cholera, dysentery, and typhoid fever. All of these diseases were caused by bacteria in the lake's water. In 1892, Chicagoans began a huge engineering project that reversed the flow of the Chicago River to protect Chicago's drinking water in Lake Michigan. However, this reversal also meant that water would be diverted from Lake Michigan at a rate of about 10,000 cubic feet (283 cu m) per second.

In 1909, the governments of Canada and the United States signed the International Boundary Waters Treaty that set up the International Joint Commission (IJC). Since then, this commission has met every two years to resolve problems regarding the use and quality of the lakes' water and to make suggestions on improving water quality. One matter that the IJC monitors is the diversion of water from the lakes, including Chicago's diversion from Lake Michigan. As of the 1990s, the U.S. courts now only allow the diversion at a rate of 3,200 cubic feet (91 cu m) per second.

During the late 1960s Lake Erie was heavily polluted by discharge from surrounding mills and factories.

Until the late 1960s, pollution continued to build up in the lakes' waters. This was especially true of Lake Erie, which was considered a dead lake. Pollution from steel mills and other factories, sewage filled with phosphorus from household detergents and fertilizers from farms that edged the lake had fouled it. Fish and plant life in the lake were dying. Smelly scum covered the lake. Beaches were closed to swimmers and boaters. In 1969 the Cuyahoga River, which drains into Lake Erie, caught fire from all the chemicals in the water. This finally moved the government to clean up the lake.

In 1972, the IJC worked out the Great Lakes Water Quality Agreement (GLWQA) between the United States and Canada. Through this treaty, limits were put on the amount of phosphorus that could be put in detergents. In turn, the amount of phosphorus discharged into all the lakes decreased. The treaty also called for a major expansion of sewage treatment systems for cities on the lakes. By the 1990s, Lake Erie's water was much improved. The beaches were reopened, and sport fishers returned to the lake. The environments of the other lakes had improved also. The population of bald eagles, cormorants, and ospreys, which had almost disappeared, began to recover.

In 1987, the GLWQA was expanded to include a list of forty-three Areas of Concern. Plans were made to clean them up. As of 2007 only two Areas of Concern—Collingwood Harbor and Severn Sound, both in Lake Huron's Georgian Bay—have been cleaned up and taken off the list.

In 1991 the governments of the United States and Canada, as well as the state and provincial governments of Minnesota, Wisconsin, Michigan, and Ontario, set up a program to stop the discharge of toxic chemicals into Lake Superior. Some progress has been made, but fishers are still told not to eat too many of some kinds of fish caught in the lake. However, several toxic chemicals, such as mercury, dioxins, and PCBs, do not break down. They continue to be threats in the lakes, poisoning fish and birds. When people, especially young children and pregnant women, eat these fish, they can become poisoned also. Mercury can cause nerve and brain damage.

WATER QUANTITY AND WATER LEVELS

At times, drier parts of the United States have looked with envy on the water of the Great Lakes. They have even proposed moving water from the Lakes through an extended canal system or by tanker ships or trucks to the desert Southwest. In 1998, a Canadian company received approval from the Province of Ontario to withdraw about 156 million gallons (590 million L) of Lake Superior water each year and ship it by tanker to Asian countries experiencing water shortages. People living along Lake Superior, as well as the governments of the states bordering the lakes, opposed this action so strongly that the plan was dropped. As a result the governors of the Great Lakes states and the premier of Ontario worked out an agreement to prevent any removal of Great Lakes water from the Great Lakes Basin.

Rally participants in Windsor, Ontario, Canada, urged the U.S. and Canadian governments to adopt a policy that would stop all pollutants from going into the Great Lakes.

Since 1997, water levels in Lakes Michigan, Huron, and Erie have dropped by about 4 feet (1.2 m). Lake Superior experienced drought conditions in the early 2000s. These drops in water level have occurred because of warmer winters and drier-than-usual summers. When water temperatures are warm, more water evaporates from the lakes. The effects of these lower lake levels are felt in many ways. A decrease in water level of only 1 inch (2.54 cm) can cause losses of several billion dollars a year for Great Lakes shipping companies. This happens because the freighters have to carry less cargo so they will not scrape bottom in shallow parts

A man wades in the shallow waters of Lake Michigan near a buoy that usually floats 2 to 3 feet higher.

of the lakes or when going through connecting rivers and canals. Marinas that shelter yachts and other pleasure boats have to dredge, or dig, deeper harbors. For these and other reasons, many Great Lakes towns and cities have water bans in place. The ability to water lawns, wash cars, and fill backyard swimming pools has been limited and in some places eliminated during the summer months.

PROTECTING SHORELINES

Every time a marina or vacation home is built, a lake's shoreline changes. Over many years, winds and waves erode the shorelines, pulling more sand back into the lakes. Since the 1990s, as the lakes' water levels have dropped, their beaches have grown wider. As a result, more grasses and other vegetation have sprouted up on the once-clear beaches. Resort, hotel, and other property owners have often removed this vegetation because it is unsightly and sometimes smelly. Such removal has caused more **erosion** and has destroyed some wildlife habitats. In 2003 the State of Michigan began passing laws to make it difficult for people to remove shoreline vegetation.

However, it is difficult for U.S. and state governments to control much of the Great Lakes shoreline. Only 20 percent of the shore on the U.S. side of the lakes is public land—used for city and state beaches; state parks; and national parks, lakeshores, and recreation areas. Private property owners—homeowners, resort, and mill owners, farmers—like to do whatever they think is best for the shore on their land. The Province of Ontario has a better chance of protecting its shoreline because the Canadian and provincial governments own 80 percent of the land.

By the 1990s and early 2000, individuals, companies, farmers, and shipowners had become aware of how fragile the Great Lakes ecosystem is. Today, Great Lakes region residents want people far into the future to enjoy the beauty and recreational opportunities of the lakes. But most of all they are working to protect the lakes' sweet water for the future generations living in the Great Lakes Basin.

The sweet waters of Lake Erie (right) ▸▸
and of all the Great Lakes are natural
treasures worth protecting.

Glossary

alkaline basic; having a pH of more than 7, such as ammonia or baking soda.

ballast water that is taken on a ship when cargo is unloaded and that is released when cargo is loaded in order to keep the ship balanced and stable

circumnavigate to go completely around something

ecology study of the relationship between plants, animals, and their environment

ecosystem community of plants, animals, and humans interacting with their natural environment

erosion wearing away of shorelines or cliffs by water or wind

exotic species plant or animal that enters a new environment; also called invasive species

lock boxlike space that fills with water to raise and lower ships as they travel along a canal from one water level to another

megalopolis long, continuous stretch of cities, suburbs, and towns that seems like one giant-size city

phytoplankton microscopic plants that float in water

portage carrying of a boat overland between bodies of water

seiche sudden surge of water caused by strong winds or by a change in air pressure that causes a large amount of water to pile up on one side of a lake

zooplankton extremely small animals that float in water

Fast Facts

Names: Lake Superior, Lake Michigan, Lake Huron, Lake Erie, Lake Ontario

Nicknames: The Inland Seas, The Fourth Coast, Sweet Water Seas

Date of completion: About 8000 B.C. at the end of the last Ice Age

Location: East-central North America, between Canada and the United States

Surface area: 94,250 square miles (244,106 sq. km)

Volume of water: 5,473 cubic miles, or 6 quadrillion U.S. gallons

Greatest distance east to west: 350 miles (563 km) on Lake Superior

Greatest distance north to south: 307 miles (494 km) on Lake Michigan

Length of coastline: 11,000 miles (17,702 km)

Bordering land: New York, Pennsylvania, Ohio, Indiana, Michigan, Illinois, Wisconsin, and Minnesota in the United States and the province of Ontario in Canada

Highest elevation: 600 feet (182 m) above sea level, on Lake Superior

Lowest elevation: 245 feet (74 m) above sea level, on Lake Ontario

Average July water temperatures: 50°F (10°C) in Lake Superior to 70°F (21°C) in Lake Erie

Average annual precipitation: 31 inches (78 cm) in Lake Superior to 36 inches (91 cm) in Lake Ontario

Population of surrounding land: 42 million

Population of largest metropolitan areas:

United States (2006)		Canada (2006)	
Chicago, Illinois	9,505,748	Toronto, Ontario	5,113,149
Detroit, Michigan	4,468,966	Hamilton, Ontario	692,911
Cleveland, Ohio	2,114,155	Oshawa, Ontario	330,594
Milwaukee, Wisconsin	1,509,981	Windsor, Ontario	323,342
Buffalo, New York	1,137,520	Kingston, Ontario	152,358

Major islands:

Manitoulin Island, Lake Huron

Isle Royale, Lake Superior

Beaver Island, Lake Michigan

Wolfe Island, Lake Ontario

Pelee Island, Lake Erie

Isle Royale, Lake Superior

Famous landmarks:

Isle Royale National Park, Lake Superior

Perry's Peace Victory and International Memorial, South Bass Island, Lake Erie

Pictured Rocks National Lakeshore, Lake Superior

Sleeping Bear Dunes, Lake Michigan

Split Rock Light, Lake Superior

Wasaga Beach, Lake Huron

CN Tower, Lake Ontario

Economy: Fishing, marinas, shipping, tourism

Famous people:

Étienne Brûlé (1592–1633), French explorer and fur trader sent west by Champlain; became first European to see Lake Superior (1622).

Samuel de Champlain (1567–1635), French explorer and founder of the city of Quebec in Canada; traveled on Lakes Huron and Ontario.

Henry Chandler Cowles (1869–1939), American botanist at the University of Chicago who founded the science of ecology.

René-Robert Cavelier, Sieur de La Salle (1643–1687), French explorer who led expeditions to Lake Ontario (1669); had *Le Griffon*, the first boat with sails on the Great Lakes, built on Lake Erie and sailed it to Green Bay in Lake Michigan (1679).

Samuel de Champlain

Jean Nicolet (1598–1642), French explorer and first-known European to arrive on Lake Michigan (1634).

Famous shipwrecks:

Le Griffon, 1679, Lake Michigan or Lake Huron

Walk-on-the Water, 1821, Lake Erie

Lady Elgin, 1860, Lake Michigan

Charles S. Price, 1913, Lake Huron

Noronic, 1949, Lake Ontario

Edmund Fitzgerald, 1975, Lake Superior

Animals: Great Lakes fish—bass, channel catfish, chub, cisco, kiyi, lake sturgeon, muskellunge, northern pike, perch, sauger, shiner, silver lamprey, smelt, stickleback, various salmon and trout, walleye, whitefish. Mammals—caribou, moose, wolf, deer, beaver. Amphibians—several varieties of frog, mudpuppy, newt, salamander, toad. Reptiles—Blanding's, bog, and painted turtles; several varieties of skink, eastern garter snake, black rat snake, eastern massasauga snake. Birds—cormorant, eagle, egret, hawks, heron, lake gull, loon, mallard duck, osprey, tern.

Caribou

Cattails

Plants: Aquatic plants—American elodea, bladderwort, cattail, common naiad, coontail, duckweed, muskgrass, clasping-leaf pondweed, curly-leaf pondweed, floating-leaf pondweed, large-leaf pondweed, sago pondweed, water milfoil, water stargrass, wild celery. Land plants—balsam fir, birch, chestnut, spruce, white oak, white pine trees; dwarf iris, goldenrod, violet wildflowers.

Greatest threats: Chemical and industrial pollution; invasive, exotic animal species, and invasive plant species.

Find Out More

....
BOOKS
....

St. Antoine, Sara (ed.). *The Great Lakes.* (Stories from Where We Live). Minneapolis: Milkweed Editions, 2005.

Stewart, Melissa. *Life in a Lake* (Ecosystems in Action). Minneapolis: Lerner Publications Company, 2003.

Volgenau, Gerry. *Islands: Great Lakes' Stories.* Ann Arbor, MI: Ann Arbor Media Group, 2005.

....
AUDIO
....

Lightfoot, Gordon. *Songbook.* Warner Brothers. CD, Disk 3 has "The Wreck of the Edmund Fitzgerald."

Murdock, Lee. *Between Two Worlds,* CD, 2004.

———. *The Lost Lake Sailors*, CD, 2000.

———. *Standing at the Wheel*, CD, 2002.

....
VIDEOS
....

The Great Lakes. Madison, WI: Hawkhill Associates, 2004. Three-part DVD, about 60 minutes long.

Great Lakes Shipwreck Disasters. Southport Video, DVD, 2001.

Great Stories of the Great Lakes. Southport Video, DVD, 2004.

WEB SITES

Great Lakes Information Network

www.great-lakes.net

Includes pages on each lake, such as current weather conditions, environment, economy, and tourism, as well as an education page with further information about the culture, history, and geography of the lakes and surrounding land.

Great Lakes Shipwreck Museum

www.shipwreckmuseum.com

Includes a virtual tour of the museum and information about the *Edmund Fitzgerald*, other shipwrecks, and the Mariners' Memorial.

Isle Royale National Park

www.nps.gov/isro

Includes pages of information on plants, animals, history, and geology of the island.

Our Great Lakes

www.on.ec.gc.ca/greatlakes/

Canadian Web site with choice of English- or French-language pages. Includes news updates, information about plants and animals, and a special kids' page. Also has links to other sites with more environmental information.

Index

Page numbers in **boldface** are illustrations and charts.

ABOUT THE AUTHOR

Patricia K. Kummer has a B.A. in history from the College of Saint Catherine in Saint Paul, Minnesota, and an M.A. in history from Marquette University in Milwaukee, Wisconsin. She has contributed chapters to several American and world history text books and has written more than sixty books about states, countries, inventions, and other topics.

During her childhood in Minnesota, Kummer visited the North Shore of Lake Superior from Duluth to Thunder Bay several times and was amazed by the Aerial Lift Bridge. Since 1967, Kummer has lived near Lake Michigan, in Milwaukee and then in Chicago. She has spent many summer afternoons on the beaches in those cities and at the beaches and sand dunes on the Michigan side of the lake. During trips to Toronto and Cleveland, she has also enjoyed the lakefronts along Ontario and Erie. Kummer is also familiar with the lakes' other bridges and interconnecting waterways. She has crossed the Ambassador Bridge from Detroit to Windsor, Ontario, and has driven along Lake Saint Clair and the Saint Clair River before visiting the Lake Huron towns of Sarnia, Ontario, and Port Huron, Michigan.

Currently, Kummer lives with her husband in a western suburb of Chicago that receives Lake Michigan's sweet water.